What Now?
A Widow's Guide to Financial Independence

Paul L. Marrella, J.D., CFP®, CLTC

DEDICATION

This book is dedicated to my mentors— my personal mentors, my parents, Paul A. and Mary Jo Marrella, and my professional mentor, the late Hon. Thomas M. Golden, all of whom constantly pushed me to be the best I could be. I also dedicate this book to my wife, Tracy, who constantly supports and motivates me to better myself.

What Now? A Widow's Guide to Financial Independence

The information contained in this book does not purport to be a complete description of the securities, markets, or developments referred to in this material. The information has been obtained from sources considered to be reliable, but we do not guarantee that the foregoing material is accurate or complete. Any information is not a complete summary or statement of all available data necessary for making an investment decision and does not constitute a recommendation. Any opinions of the chapter authors are those of the chapter author. Expressions of opinion are as of the initial book publishing date and are subject to change without notice. All financial, retirement and estate planning should be individualized as each person's situation is unique. This information is not intended as a solicitation or an offer to buy or sell any security referred to herein. Keep in mind that there is no assurance that our recommendations or strategies will ultimately be successful or profitable nor protect against a loss. There may also be the potential for missed growth opportunities that may occur after the sale of an investment. Recommendations, specific investments or strategies discussed may not be suitable for all investors. Past performance may not be indicative of future results. Please note, changes in laws may occur at any time and could have a substantial impact upon each person's situation. While we are familiar with the provisions of the issues presented herein, as financial advisors we are not qualified to render advice on tax or legal matters.

You should discuss any tax or legal matters with the appropriate professional. Information should not be considered a recommendation of the advisor's services or abilities, or indicate a favorable client experience. The experiences described here may not be representative of any future experience of our clients. Individual results will vary.

ACKNOWLEDGEMENTS

This book would not have been possible without the tireless help of my business advisors, John Bowen, Sharla Hamil and Sydney LeBlanc.

PROLOGUE

I grew up in the house of a financial advisor. Unlike most kids, when I came in from playing kick ball, "Wall Street Week" was on TV. Early on, I developed an affinity for the financial markets. My parents grew up with very limited financial resources, and stressed the importance of hard work and making sound financial decisions. In fact, poor financial decisions were unacceptable. This stuck with me for a long time.

When I was in law school, I commuted 70 miles every day to work in my father's financial planning business. What I noticed there was the value of people making sound long-term financial decisions. A good financial decision-maker tended to have more wealth than not. This art form seems to be absent in today's world.

As a young attorney, I quickly realized 90% of my job was solving people's problems. Many of them could have been prevented with proper planning, saving time, money and aggravation. Understanding, identifying and preventing the potential complications in advance is a far more valuable skill than being able to fix them. My legal career taught me that knowing the right questions to ask is far more important than their answers.

After my legal career, I followed a childhood dream and worked as a Wall Street Stock Trader. On a daily basis, I witnessed the emotional effects money has on people, and some of the irrational behavior that resulted.

Getting "caught in the moment" and making poor decisions were incredibly destructive and costly. We had an old saying: "First loss, best loss," meaning that when you are wrong, fix the problem right away, rather than allowing a minor bad decision to snowball into a disaster.

Today, I am fortunate to be able to use my diverse professional experiences helping clients plan their and their families' financial futures. I help them identify their financial goals as well as potential problems they may face. The real-world benefit is to act as my clients' Personal Financial Coach, helping them make prudent, well-thought, objective financial decisions so they can make the most of their hard-earned money, just like my parents did for me.

PREFACE: WHY I WROTE THIS BOOK

"Life is really simple, but we insist on making it complicated."
– Confucius

Years ago, many of my friends used to joke, "What do you do, manage 'little old ladies' money?" They all thought it was strange when I answered "Yes, they aren't all little, nor are they old, but that is what I do." In my title, I included the word "widow" yet, through poetic license, I intended a looser definition. To help more of you, I included guidance for both women who unfortunately have lost their spouses ("traditional widows"), *and* women concerned about managing their financial affairs in case they survive their spouses ("could be widows"). Please do not interpret any of this book as sexist; in fact, many men could benefit from reading it. My last caveat is that I wrote this book on a basic level, hoping that anyone could benefit from reading it. I simply want you to know the questions to ask so you can achieve all that is important to you…and your family.

When I decided to write my book, I had several goals in mind. I wanted to:

- Inform you, the reader, of what to expect, and what you'll have to do if, and when, a beloved spouse predeceases you
- Educate you on what you will need to accomplish, so you have the confidence to manage your future financial affairs
- Help you learn from others' mistakes, so you don't make them yourself
- Help you understand why planning is so important, and to appreciate how proper planning can help prevent future problems
- Show you how to simplify your financial affairs, and offer this book as a reference tool so you can do so
- Illustrate how you can make your decision-making less emotional

I am confident that, after reading this book, I can help you and your financial advisor make sound financial decisions. Managing your wealth comes down to plain old, good decision-making; and you can't make too many good decisions.

Who Benefits From the Book?

I believe three primary groups can benefit from this book. First is the widow who recently lost her spouse. This book is designed to guide and inform you, and let you know what to expect, both emotionally and financially. I want you to think about some of the decisions you have to make, and how you can get help making them.

Married women who do not handle the financial responsibilities and are concerned about surviving their spouse are in the second group who can benefit from the book. More and more, I have women come to my office wanting to engage me as an advisor. Their concern is out-living their spouse and needing an advisor later. They want to be educated, and to proactively plan so their affairs are in order if their husband predeceases them. I am told this provides confidence.

The third group includes couples who want to start planning. More and more, I see the financial spouse engage us as a client, knowing that when they pass away their spouse will be taken care of; they want to engage a skilled professional to advise their spouse. This book can be used as a tool to open the discussion of planning.

Table of Contents

INTRODUCTION

"Never be afraid to raise your voice for honesty and truth and compassion against injustice and lying and greed. If people all over the world...would do this, it would change the earth."

—William Faulkner

As a young attorney, I had the opportunity to work for a great lawyer and mentor. One of the most valuable lessons he taught me happened by accident. The case involved a young mother who suddenly lost her husband, a local businessman with several partners. Fortunately, he planned properly, and had a valid buy-sell agreement so his wife could easily sell his business interests. The problem was that his partners were not honoring this contract; instead, they were trying to short-change her.

I had been in my boss' office for a "teaching moment" when he received a call. I knew it was something important when he asked me to close the door. What started as a friendly conversation quickly turned adversarial and loud. His faced turned red, and his voice got louder and his language more decisive; expletives were flying. "This is wrong!!" he shouted, "That is unacceptable! If you don't have a reasonable offer to me by noon tomorrow, I will have you in court, and your client wants no parts of that!" It was a full-blown shouting match.

My first thought was, "What kind of career did I get myself into?" When the conversation ended, he took me aside, as he often did, and explained that he does not usually conduct himself that way with others, including other attorneys. In this case, he had no choice. He could not, and would not, stand for these partners' unacceptable behavior. He made it very clear that his job was to be her advocate; his job was to protect her interests and solve a problem she did not know she had.

I am sure the woman never knew what happened in his office that day; only that she was dealt with fairly. I will never forget what he did, and how much he helped solve her problem. I realized at that moment why he was such a successful attorney. It was simple: he helped solve people's problems and looked out for their best interests. I still wonder how many people just like her, not lucky enough to have an advocate, are taken advantage of every day. I vowed that day to act as my clients' advocate, first as an attorney, and now as their financial advisor.

During any given day, I help a number of people just like the woman in my story. Throughout the years, I've interviewed, met with, and advised hundreds of women. I think women are underserved and are a misunderstood demographic. I want to share my 20-plus years' experience as an attorney, Wall Street trader and financial advisor, to illustrate what you can do to preserve your financial interests, to make better decisions and to get help when needed.

CHAPTER ONE: WHAT WIDOWS WANT AND NEED…. BUT DON'T ALWAYS GET

"A smart man makes a mistake, learns from it, and never makes that mistake again. But a wise man finds a smart man and learns from him how to avoid the mistake altogether."

—Roy H. Williams, Author

Widows' (and, in many cases, women's) challenges are very common, which makes me wonder why this group is so underserved. While doing my research, I was surprised to find that many women are treated poorly by financial professionals. A Boston Consulting Group Study[1] discussed the condescending attitude and the lack of advice given to women. Maybe that's why 70% leave their advisors once widowed. The study also noted this was peculiar considering that women are willing to accept advice and have the potential to be great clients for advisors.

Women are a major force in the financial world. They manage a significant sum of assets and according to an article by the Boston Consulting Group[2], women are sole heads of 32% of the world's wealth, which is expected to grow in the coming years.Why would widows be such a substantial group of consumers and fail to get sound, professional advice? I believe the answer lies in the failure to understand what widows want and need.

First and foremost, what widows need is a trusted advisor. They also need and want the following:

- They want someone who will be compassionate and capable.
- They need to understand not only what needs to be done but "why," and so they need to be educated.
- They want to be able to ask the right questions.
- They need ongoing, competent advice.
- They want a long-term relationship with their advisor, not short-term fixes soon after their husband dies.
- They need a relationship with a point person, a business coach and someone they can rely on for years to come; they do not want a salesperson.

Most importantly, what widows need, and may not know it, is an Advocate. An Advocate understands, and weeds through all the Wall Street jargon and hype, and provides solutions their clients can understand. An Advocate helps their clients make sound financial decisions today that will make a positive impact on their and their family's future. In essence, widows need a personal "Financial Coach."

Often overlooked is that women really want an advisor who will listen to them. They want to be heard, they want their goals established, and they want someone they can communicate and be comfortable with; they want an advisor who will guide them.

From all of my interviews, I was repeatedly told, the most underrated aspect of what people want is to keep things simple. They really just want to know "what time it is," they don't want to know "how to make a clock." Too often, financial professionals tend to use industry slang instead of using simple English. Furthermore, advisors need to explain the "why" of their advice. When we simplify financial language and strategies so that anyone can understand it, it gives them confidence that they're making informed decisions. I can't stress that enough.

Financial independence is our clients' most common goal. We define financial independence as being able to maintain your current lifestyle, without having to work and without relying on others for financial help. Understanding when you have reached financial independence can be difficult and requires considerable planning. This is especially important for widows who have not historically made the financial decisions for their family.

In most families, only one spouse handles the money and the investment decisions. According to a UBS Study, "Own your worth[3]," only about 44% of the women in this country handle the investments and financial planning. If the investment-handling spouse passes first, it creates a lot of difficulty for the surviving spouse. Most times, that's a woman or the widow because women are 3.5 times as likely to survive their husbands based on a *Barron's* article, "Widowed Women Highlight Wealth Gap Between Genders".[4]

It is my hope that this book will clearly establish what a surviving spouse needs to do to be successful financially. When reading this book, note some of the concerns you want addressed, and consider which advisor can fulfill them. Hopefully, you will have a better idea of what you can expect.

CHAPTER TWO: EMOTION RELATED ISSUES

"The one permanent emotion of the inferior man is fear - fear of the unknown, the complex, the inexplicable. What he wants above everything else is safety."
—H. L. Mencken, scholar

Be Aware of Emotional Issues

There is nothing in life more emotional than losing a loved one. It can affect you in a number of ways. When a woman becomes a widow, she will face making many new decisions; some that will have long-term ramifications. As a widow, you need to re-establish your priorities, placing YOUR interests first, not the interests of others. For most widows, this can be overwhelming. But emotions are important and need to be understood.

Why is emotion so important? Emotion is what separates humans from the rest of the animal kingdom. It's hard-wired into us, something that allows us to live in a society. It allows us to care for other's feelings, and it allows us to be more civil than the wild animals. Emotions are wide-ranging. They're sometimes positive, they're sometimes negative, and they affect people differently. Emotions also tend to be strong. We're dealing with the two most emotional things that exist in people's lives: their loved ones and their money.

When you lose a loved one, emotional issues are magnified to an extent that most people haven't encountered until they experience it themselves. Everybody responds differently to these emotions, which could be devastating when you're trying to manage your other affairs. Once again, my recommendation is to seek help. It could be a psychologist, support group or network, spiritual advisor, your children, friends, colleagues, or neighbors. It's very important that widows, in particular, truly comprehend the emotional impacts they will face. Knowing what to expect may allow you to better handle the effects of these emotions.

Anticipating and understanding emotions well ahead of time, and some of the mistakes people make as a result, might help you make better decisions. Furthermore, delegating the mounds of paperwork to a professional will be far less painful for you, and may help expedite the process.

Grief

Grief is probably the most common emotion, especially after losing a loved one; I don't think you'd be human if you didn't express this emotion. Suddenly, money becomes less of a priority and your healing becomes the top priority. In a lot of cases, this can result in denial and even the rejecting of an inheritance. Sometimes it results in "investment paralysis." Investment paralysis basically means "doing nothing." The shock of loss is so great that people just don't want to deal with anything. I can think of several cases where women have come to me several years after their husband's death with a stack of paperwork saying, "I have all these things and nothing has been updated. Can you help?"

In one instance, a woman contacted me three years after her husband had passed. She had done nothing with his IRA which was still in his name, and had not taken his Required Minimum Distributions (An annual IRS mandatory retirement plan withdrawal). The IRS imposed statutory penalty for not taking theses withdrawals is 50% of the required withdrawal amount. She learned a valuable, but expensive, lesson on the possible negative impact of deferring decisions.

Guilt

Guilt is another emotion that many people do not expect after the loss of a spouse. Especially guilt as it relates to money. A financial gain can be the result of loss, for example, receiving money from an insurance settlement or a husband's pension or savings. Oftentimes, a widow will experience guilt thinking that spending the money is like saying it was okay that her husband died. In other instances, women may think that their spouse saved and sacrificed all those years and they just can't enjoy the money now that the spouse is gone. (See Emotional Attachment below.) Again, this prolongs the decision-making timeframe. Many times, we see assets or securities left unmanaged because they want to "honor" the spouse. This is usually not the best decision.

Emotional Attachment

I talk to many widows who want to manage their money exactly "how daddy did it." In some cases, their husbands may have told them how they should manage the money for the long term. This may not be a good long term plan because the financial world is sure to change. Sometimes, they feel they want to hang on to the assets that made them wealthy. That happens frequently with stock held in the company the husband worked for, or a family business. However, there is always the possibility that even seemingly sound companies and their respective stock can experience severe downturns at any time.

The consequences of making this potential mistake can be life-changing. Rarely does this emotional attachment make sense and, oftentimes, it breaks all the rules of prudent investment management.

Loneliness

Loneliness, or the isolation felt after losing a spouse, is another common emotion when a widow does not know where to get proper advice. This frequently happens when widows have no children. One potential problem is that lonely people are more susceptible to being scammed.

I once received a call from a client who was asked by an elderly, widowed friend to help review her mail. My client wanted to know why her friend's investment account was registered with her attorney (and agent under the friend's power of attorney) jointly with right of survivorship. This meant that upon the friend's death, the entire account would be transferred by operation of law to her attorney/agent. The attorney/agent, incidentally, was not a family member.

My client was confused why this would have happened because she did not think this was how her friend would have wanted such a large part of her estate transferred. Soon thereafter, I referred the case to a local attorney who then contacted the Berks County Office of Aging for resolution. Ultimately, the attorney/agent was disbarred for five years.[5]

In no way is this story meant to disparage the legal profession (of which I am a member). Instead, I want you to understand what can happen without proper representation, both financially, legally and by your agent named in your power of attorney. Sadly, this type of situation probably occurs far more often than we want to think.

Paranoia

In some cases wealth creates new friends. Unfortunately, widows can become targets of friends, family, and charities all looking for a piece of the pie. The result is that widows may become overly suspicious and will tend to separate themselves from these types of people and society, creating isolation and abandoning healthy long-time relationships. Determining boundaries right from the "get-go" and having a professional assist you is very important.

Know What you Don't Know

As if emotional issues are not enough, you must still anticipate what will happen when you must confront your financial planning. If you do not have experience managing finances, professional help may be a good way to sort them out so you can understand them. You may also need some basic education so you can understand the gravity of managing your finances and investments. Always remember, a little knowledge can be dangerous.

Feeling Overwhelmed by Financial Issues

Feeling overwhelmed is also a common feeling that is wide-ranging. Think about it: you're grieving the loss of a loved one, and you have to deal with a mound of paperwork you don't understand. Most people don't know where to begin, and have a fear they might miss something important that they're not aware of. Some women are just plain terrified of handling their money for the first time.

If your life partner made your decisions all these years, and now you must make the decisions by yourself, it will be overwhelming. Some of you may not know how to manage finances because you never had to; I have known widows who never even wrote a check. Many of my widow clients have told me they don't know how much money comes in on a monthly basis and how much they need to pay for the daily living expenses, taxes and major bills they will face. This is a lot to learn and comprehend, especially in the face of having lost a spouse.

Confusion

I don't think there are many businesses more guilty of this than on Wall Street. I hate to say it, but my profession makes things far too complicated. I'm not sure if Wall Street firms do this to make the firms look smart, whether they try to confuse people, or perhaps to justify their fees. When complicated financial concepts are explained in a simplified manner, clients can more quickly comprehend them. When a client has an understanding of the implications of their decisions, it gives them a much greater confidence to do the things they want to do. This helps all investors, not just widows, but is so very important at all stages of investing and planning. Life is complicated enough and we shouldn't try to make it harder than it is.

Procrastination

Many times, procrastination is the primary stumbling block when it comes to finding an advisor. Think about these things: If you don't have an advisor, where would you go for help? If you do, can you trust that advisor to act as your Advocate and to function as your Personal Financial Coach? Does it make sense to get a second opinion? There's nothing we can do about yesterday; all we can do is take what we know, build on that knowledge, and apply it to ourselves so we can make good decisions in the future.

As you're reading this book, I would like you to do a few things so procrastination won't be an issue for you. First, you need to identify your goals. If you're now widowed, ask yourself what you want your wealth to do for you. Is it to provide a desired or confident retirement? Is it to educate grandkids? Do you think you have enough to accomplish these goals? What happens if you need long term care?

While the various emotional issues detailed above might seem trivial, their effects are not. Increased emotion typically results in a loss of objectivity. The natural tendency is to make decisions that will relieve the pain today, rather than what might be best for you and your family in future years. Have you ever heard anyone say, "I don't know what I was thinking?" Securing objective, professional advice today may result in fewer problems down the road.

CHAPTER THREE: ENEMIES OF MEETING YOUR GOALS

"I've had nonstop financial problems my whole adult life. It's always been a constant balance, year to year: 'Where's the time? Where's the money?'"
—Lorrie Moore, American Novelist

My experience is that after a few months, widows focus on the long term with their money, which is a good thing. Typically, maintaining a comfortable retirement is their top financial priority. They're not always worried about how much they accumulate or how fast it grows. Many times, they are more interested in how much they need to take care of themselves and their families.[6] The disconnect here is that while most people know what they want, they have difficulty understanding how to get there, and what are their challenges or obstacles that get in the way. Whether you are a widow or any individual considering retirement, or thinking about financial independence, there are five primary enemies of meeting your goals. They are: debt, emotional bias, longevity, inflation, and future medical costs. I'll outline each one of them individually.

Debt

Why is debt so bad? The problem with debt is that it takes away from the valuable monthly cash flow people need. While you're working, you receive your pay check regularly (i.e., every week, every other week), you know how much it will be, and you can budget around it. When you retire, or if you suddenly become a widow, the cash flows you are accustomed to will be changed or may even end.

Once a regular monthly income is gone, it must be replaced. And, any time you have debt in retirement, it takes away from this monthly income. The existence of debt results in a bill and increases the amount of income that you need in order to live and pay your debt. Whether you're a recent widow or you're in the planning process, you need to identify the following:

- How much debt do you have?
- How much money would it take to pay off all the debt?
- Do you have a plan to reduce the debt? If so, how?
- When will the debt be paid off?

Debt repayment can be planned for and managed. Nonetheless, debt is one of the bigger problems people face in retirement or when facing the death of a spouse. I always advise clients to be debt-free prior to retiring.

Longevity

Longevity is a major concern for widows. Based on the 2020 Retirement and Survivor Benefits Life Expectancy[7] calculator from Social Security Administration[8], here are some facts that are sobering:

- The average 55-year-old female will live 30.1 years
- The average 65-year-old female will live 21.2 years
- The average 75-year-old female will live 13.2 years
- The average 85-year-old female will live 7.0 years

According to this Social Security Administration Calculator, a 65-year old male will live approximately 18.7 more years, which is about 2.5 years less than the female. This is yet another reason women need to think about their future independence if they lose a spouse.

If that's not concerning enough, remember that average means half of those people will die before those estimates and half of them will live even longer, well past those estimates. Think about when you last attended the funeral of a 65-year-old? Did you think to yourself, "Boy, he was so young." We see our 90 year old clients getting heart bypass surgery, for example, and other medical procedures the medical profession wouldn't have even considered 20 years ago.

Taking the longevity factor into consideration, planning is more important than ever today. Even though significantly more planning is required, which results in greater time demands, we're looking at longer retirements and greater needs for assets. My profession now plans for 30- and 40-year retirements rather than for 10 or 15-year retirements that we planned for a few years ago. And the reason it is more time-consuming is because financial issues have become more complicated.

Emotional Bias

How do emotions play a role in your decision-making process? How can they derail your goals? There are many types of emotions (and we outlined the most common personal types in the previous chapter) that widows may face and they can affect your decision-making. Emotional bias, however, is a distortion in the cognition in decision-making that comes from emotional factors. Simply put, people are reluctant to accept facts that are unpleasant and create mental suffering. In essence, they want to avoid what feels bad and do what feels good. The result is, what you want is probably going to be completely different than what you *need.* Think about when you see and smell chocolate chip cookies. We all know, chocolate chip cookies aren't the most nutritious food but, boy, do they taste good. We all know that we don't need them to survive, but we want them because it makes us feel better, even if only temporarily.

This happens all too often in the financial world; sometimes people want to hang on to a company's stock because their spouse worked at the company their entire work life and it has financially rewarded them. What they *want* is an investment that is familiar to them, one that feels "comfortable." What they *need* is diversification, although diversification does not ensure a profit or guarantee against a loss. Sometimes people *want* certainty, but what they really *need* is to take prudent investment risk. What you want is not always what you need. The stronger these emotions are, the more difficult it is to make objective decisions. That's part of the problem with handling your own money – people lose objectivity.

At the end of the day, the greatest obstacles that widows face are their own biases and choices, not the complex finances, not the math of inflation and longevity.

Inflation

"Inflation is as violent as a mugger, as frightening as an armed robber and as deadly as a hit man."
—Ronald Reagan

A retiree's greatest enemy is inflation, and it goes hand-in-hand with longevity. What you have to do is plan on the fact that everything will cost you more in the future than it does today. Think back to the year you graduated high school— how much did a car or an ice cream cost? Significantly less than they do today. Think about things like your homeowner's insurance or your property taxes, how they've escalated in recent years. We have to be concerned, not just about what things cost today, but what they will cost well into the future. If you plan on spending $4,000 per month today, how much will you need in the future? If inflation were to continue at 3% then, in theory, you can expect the need to double your monthly **income** to $8,000 after 24 years of retirement. Understanding the basics of inflation is critically important to all widows.

You can see on Chart 1 that follows how your everyday spending will increase in the future. Adding to the problem, most pensions do not increase with inflation. Unfortunately, fewer and fewer people today have pensions. Social Security benefits increase according to the consumer price index today (COLA - Cost of Living Adjustment), but with all the Social Security funding problems, these increases may not continue in the future. If all these costs increase in the future and your income stays the same, or your assets remain unchanged, how are you going to pay your bills? As a widow, you need to make sure that you plan for the negative effects of inflation, along with what everybody wants— and that's a long, healthy life.

Chart 1: Historical and Future "Everyday" Costs

Common Expenses	1990	2020	2050*
Gallon Unleaded Regular Gasoline	$1.02	$2.27	$5.51
White Bread (per lb.)	$0.69	$1.35	$3.42
1 Dozen Large Grade A Eggs	$1.22	$2.02	$4.90
Postage Stamp	$0.25	$0.55	$1.33

Sources: US Department of Labor, Bureau of Labor Statistics (https://data.bls.gov/cgi-bin/surveymost?ap); United States Postal Service.)

* *Assumes 3% annual inflation adjustment*

Medical Costs

Healthcare coverage is essential because medical problems are both costly and unexpected. Overall healthcare costs are projected to grow 5.5% annually through 2028 according to the Peter G. Peterson Foundation.[9] A study from Fidelity Investments states that "a 65-year old couple retiring in 2019 can expect to spend $285,000 in health care and medical expenses throughout retirement... For single retirees, the health care cost estimate is $150,000 for women and $135,000 for men."[10] While Medicare helps, it will probably cover two-thirds of your medical costs according to the Employee Benefit Research Institute[11], and that does not include premiums, deductibles, co- pays, and what you may need to pay for long-term care. What some of my clients also experience is that Medicare does not cover dental, vision or hearing expenses which add up as you age.

Highlighting these "Enemies" illustrates the importance of making smart decisions today. You have to spend wisely, you have to manage your investments properly, hopefully in vehicles that will pace inflation, and most importantly, you have to avoid catastrophic financial mistakes. To help you avoid financial mistakes and help you make smart decisions, financial planning is your next step in the process. If you are a widow, the next few chapters will be of particular interest to you.

CHAPTER FOUR: BASICS OF FINANCIAL PLANNING

"Fortune favors the prepared mind."
—Louis Pasteur

Proper long-term planning is critical. For example, I once met with a widow whose husband had recently passed. As a widow, she wasn't sure about the planning her husband had done. When I contacted her husband's pension board, we confirmed that, for her lifetime, she would receive 100% of her husband's pension. As you can imagine, she was so elated, and truly relieved; it appeared the weight of the world came off her shoulders. Her income would be exactly the same tomorrow as it was the day before he had passed. Can you imagine how different our meeting would have been had he not provided a pension survivorship benefit? The value of proper planning can benefit you for many years to come.

Many times, widows need help with this basic planning which then progresses to financial planning and wealth management. This is daunting if they have no one to help. Widows are generally terrified of what lies ahead of them if they were not involved in the financial decision-making before their spouse passed. Making matters worse is they don't realize how making major mistakes will affect them for the rest of their life.

While the lack of financial education is a major problem, it can be compounded by not asking for help to understand all of the issues. This usually results in hasty decisions. Many women are so overwhelmed emotionally and financially, they just want to finalize the issues and have them taken care of in the quickest possible way. Unfortunately, this scenario makes widows easy targets for unscrupulous "salespeople."

How do you create a financial plan? The first thing you must do is add up all of your predictable sources of income today and in the future, and then you have to decide how much you think you will need to maintain your lifestyle. There are basic expenses like utilities, mortgage/rent, entertainment, clothing, insurance premiums, energy, food. These things don't change a whole lot, day-to-day or month-to-month, but will increase significantly from year-to-year.

In addition to the more recognizable expenses listed above, you need to add in the irregular and less predictable expenses. These expenses include things like new cars, major appliances (that will break), and major repairs to your home. All of these are costly and will impact even the best budgets. None of these items last forever and some of them tend to be quite expensive, and often need replacing at exactly the wrong time. What else can you think of that should be on this list that might impact your budget and income?

Many times what you don't know can be the real culprit and can really foul up your financial plan. In creating a detailed financial plan, we have to estimate these costs. It is difficult to do on your own; again, a reason to get some help.

Long-Term Care as Part of a Financial Plan

Another major financial planning matter is the issue of long-term care. I hear all the time that widows don't want to be a burden on their kids or anyone else. Sometimes, as widows age, long-term care comes into play. It's difficult to project how much someone is going to need and what it's going to cost. You must also factor in the emotional aspect as well.

Long-term care is something you need to plan for. The one sure thing is if you do need care, and it's of any reasonable duration, it's going to be expensive. According to the Genworth 2019[12] Cost of Care Survey at least 7 out of 10 people over 65 will need long-term care services at some point in their lifetime. In 2019, a private room in nursing facilities in the state of Pennsylvania averages $124,830 per year.

There are four primary types of long-term care. First, there is adult day care, where you are dropped off at the day care facility at 9:00 am and picked up at 5:00 pm; it's really not much different than how you might view child day care. The next type of care is called home healthcare which offers nurses or aides who come into your home to provide help with activities of daily living such as bathing, dressing, and eating. The third type is assisted living. Assisted living allows you to live independently but you're in a safer environment and people are watching over you, making sure that you're safe. The fourth and last type of long term-care is skilled nursing care which is provided at nursing homes.

In conclusion, most times living a long life requires having a lot of money. If you have just enough or not nearly enough, and you're fortunate enough to live a long life, you may have to live some of your later years with significantly less income than you hoped, or rely on family members for help. Failing to plan only magnifies this problem. Starting early and getting professional help are the two best ways to try to manage financial shortfalls in your retirement.

CHAPTER FIVE: WHERE DO I START?

"Basically, our goal is to organize the world's information and to make it universally accessible and useful."
—Larry Page, Co-Founder, Google

What is the first thing you have to do? If you're recently widowed, you need to gather and organize all of your information. You will have to piece your financial life together, which will require you to assemble a number of financial documents, many of which will be foreign to you. The end goal is to determine what assets you have and consolidate them in a way that you can understand them.

Some people like to see everything on a single sheet of paper, although doing so is sometimes easier said than done. In terms of gathering all the documents, you will assemble together, piece by piece, all of your financial statements. Years ago, everything came in the U.S. mail. In the electronic age, much of the information is sent electronically through email or stored in secure online databanks, each requiring a specific username and password. Password lists, if you can find them, can be pages long since people have many different electronic accounts. It's crucial that you document your various log-ons and passwords as well as your email addresses. Your spouse's electronic information is crucial as well. If you don't have everything you need to obtain all of the information electronically, you might have to go through substantial legal action to retrieve them. Having access to your spouse's email account(s) before you become a widow will be useful for many months or years to make sure all of the account information has been retrieved.

Additional records you will need are recent income tax returns. Why you ask? They're probably the best single information source for your financial affairs because they list every account that generates taxable income or expenses. You will also need multiple copies of death certificates since each financial institution will require an original. Financial statements will also be important, not just information from websites, but the actual printed statements from the banks, brokerage firms, and employer retirement plans. The reason these statements are so important is because they list things like the legal owner's name, or the registration of the accounts, the type of account, account number, the service provider's contact information, as well as account holdings and balances. This will give you enough information to analyze for yourself or for your financial professional.

Another great resource is the spouse's employer's human resources department. In my experience, these people are extremely helpful, both while your spouse is working and well into retirement. They tend to know the system, and in many cases, they know you or your spouse personally, so they can provide a variety of useful information.

There are many employee benefits people are entitled to. They include employer-sponsored arrangements like 401K plans, Profit Sharing Plans, stock option plans, and pensions. Sometimes there is retiree health insurance or current employee health insurance you are entitled to. Oftentimes, employees have life insurance through their employers if they're still working; and in many cases even in retirement. Corporate executives often have deferred compensation plans, employee stock option plans, employee stock ownership plans (ESOP Plans), and even stock appreciation rights (SARs). HR departments are a great resource and I suggest you make that one of your first few contacts. In terms of the employer plans listed above, many times there's a written contract between the employer and the employee that your spouse may have and that should be in your files.

Estate Planning Attorneys and CPAs

In many cases, family attorneys have well-documented files with details on estate plans, as well as any tax and business planning the client may have formalized. I find that attorneys are a wealth of information and, in many cases, people have enjoyed long-standing relationships with them. Typically, accountants, tax preparers and CPAs also have considerable information since they often have financial and tax statements in their computer systems.

Social Security

The Social Security Administration (www.ssa.gov, 800-772-1213) will help spouses determine their benefits, when they can collect them, and whether they are entitled to a Spousal Benefit. The general rule in retirement is that the surviving spouse gets the higher of her or her deceased spouse's benefits. (More Social Security information is discussed in the following chapter.)

Small Business Matters

If your spouse owned a small business or a privately held business, you will need to ask a few questions in order to make decisions for the business. For example, who is legally allowed to run the business, who can sign the checks, and who is authorized to sign any documents? If no one is permitted to do so, including yourself or any members of the family, you may have to go to court to appoint a guardian to run the business' affairs. This is a costly and emotional process that can be avoided with minimal planning.

Other issues you need to consider are who is capable to run the business on a day-to-day basis, and who is on the management team? If you are in the planning process, please know you cannot afford to have a poorly organized or managed business with minimal or inaccurate documents. The potential exists to bankrupt the business. Hopefully, there's been some planning done, whether it's a buy-sell agreement (funded or unfunded by life insurance), or there is a shareholders' agreement between two or more people. Nonetheless, some of these questions need to be answered.

If the business needs to be sold to keep it as an ongoing concern, you will have to consult advisors and other professionals, such as attorneys and accountants. These business and tax matters can be complicated, and the issues you may face are beyond the scope of this book.

List of Documentation

Check out the information Chart 2 following that lists the documents you should locate to determine what your assets are. These are all involved in your overall estate planning. If you have any of the following items, be sure to gather them in a file.

Chart 2: Important Financial Planning Documents
• Last two years of income tax returns
• Recent financial statements prepared for refinancing
• Current bank statements
• Current mutual fund statements
• Current brokerage statements
• Current dividend reinvestment plans statements
• Stock certificates
• Mortgage statements
• Current life, disability, and long term care insurance policies
• Current auto/ home owner's insurance policies
• Current employee benefit statements including 401K retirement plans
• Employee benefit agreements and/or handbook
• Monthly bills/utilities/credit cards
• Deeds to properties
• Business shareholder agreements, buy/sell agreements
• Wills or trust documents
• Recent credit reports

Estate Administration

After you've compiled a list of your assets, many of them will need to be transferred to you individually. In U.S. property law, every asset has a rightful owner. For larger assets, such as real estate and autos, our government tracks the "title" of them to prevent them from being transferred improperly. When the owner of an asset dies, it may be transferred in a number of ways. The law provides account registrations that will bypass some legal channels and automatically transfer title at death. So, the titling of the assets is very important.

One way assets can be transferred is by what's called "Operation of Law." In that case, all you will need is a death certificate to re-register that asset. Married couples tend to register their assets in a couple of ways: either as Joint Tenants with Right of Survivorship, or Joint Tenants by the Entireties. If that's the case, title to those assets transfers immediately at death to the surviving spouse.

Payable on Death ("POD") or Transfer on Death ("TOD") accounts are becoming more and more popular. These accounts avoid probate, and are transferred directly to the person listed on the POD registration by Operation of Law. Usually, only a death certificate is required to transfer ownership of a POD account to a surviving spouse.

Certain assets allow specific beneficiary designations to be created. These include life insurance, Individual Retirement Accounts (IRAs), Roth IRAs, qualified retirement plans, 401K plans and pension plans. These beneficiary designations supersede what the person's will states. For example, if Joe is the beneficiary listed on my life insurance policy, and my Will says my assets pass to Lucy, Joe still receives the policy proceeds. Proper planning requires that, if permitted, all such accounts should have properly named primary and contingent beneficiaries. If no beneficiary is named, the money is payable to the estate. For the "qualified retirement plans" listed above, a surviving spouse properly named as beneficiary has the option to make a transfer to their IRA which is relatively simple. Younger widows may need to create a special "Beneficiary IRA" allowing them to make penalty-free withdrawals prior to age 59 ½.

All too often, I find that there are assets registered in a deceased spouse's name individually, rather than with their spouse as joint tenants with right of survivorship. Transferring individual assets to the surviving spouse isn't as easy as people might think. In order to do so, the individual must go through a process called probate.

Probate is a process that allows people to transfer their wealth to another person. This is usually done through a will. During the probate process, a designated fiduciary (either an Executor or Administrator) is responsible to pay all the debts of the deceased person. This fiduciary would pay any outstanding debts and taxes, handle the asset transfers, then distribute the assets to their rightful heirs. This entire formal process is overseen by a probate court. The problem is it can be an expensive process. Typically, a lawyer is needed, there's a time delay, and it's a lot of unnecessary work. If you are in the planning process, spouse to spouse transfers can be established with very little time, effort and paperwork. Properly registering your and your spouse's accounts is all that is required to avoid this problem.

Occasionally, there are estate or inheritance tax reasons to register assets individually but, many times, it is just a lack of knowledge or oversight. One example I observed was when some life insurance companies demutualized and gave stock to their policyholders. MetLife, Prudential and John Hancock (now Manulife) all gave their individual policyholders shares of stock, but did so without adding a spouse on the registration. When the policyholder dies, the company often requires a formal probate process to transfer this stock to the surviving spouse, costing time and money. Again, a little planning can go a long way.

Assets which cannot transfer by Operation of Law will be passed either through the spouse's will or a process called Intestacy. Intestacy simply means dying without a will, in which case state law determines who your beneficiaries are, and may not match your wishes. For intestate estates, an Administrator is named to transfer the assets and handle the estate of the deceased party. If there is a Will, an executor is designated who is responsible to transfer the assets.

In my experience, proper planning and correctly titling your assets early on prevents many of the problems associated with the probate process for the first spouse. In addition, probate is not private; all of your estate information is free for the public to see. This is important to know especially if you value privacy. Believe me when I tell you that someone who has a bad experience in this area won't ever forget it, and will make sure that their planning doesn't fall through the cracks again.

An important note about today's privacy laws is that every transaction has to be documented in writing and attested to versus doing things over the phone like we could years ago. This greatly increases the time required to transfer these assets, because every financial institution needs written authorization to even speak to you about your spouse's money. Again, this is very difficult to do on your own and having an experienced advisor to guide you through the process can save significant time and trouble.

CHAPTER SIX: FINANCIAL NEEDS

"You have to risk failure to succeed. The important thing is not to make one single mistake that will jeopardize the future."
—Dr. An Wang, Inventor and Co-founder of Wang Laboratories

By now you've determined what assets you own and you have a net worth statement. You also have determined your sources of regular income and have some form of income statement. You need to ask yourself where are you today and where do you want to go? This task will allow you to comprehend what all these "numbers on the page" really mean. At this point, you should be ready to have a meaningful conversation with a professional about your financial goals (i.e., financial independence) and what is important to you.

The key is to fill in the gaps on how you can get there. Many people at this stage are frustrated because all they really have are account balances. What appeared like all the money in the world 20 years ago, may not be nearly enough today with the longevity and inflation. You need to determine what has to be done for you to properly plan for your future and to know exactly what situation of life you're in at the moment. Even if a widow is the one who handled the finances, she still faces an overwhelming range of emotions. This creates a lack of objectivity and, again, the inclination to make decisions on what feels good, and not what is truly needed. We'll talk about some short-term and long-term planning considerations; so hopefully, you can get a handle on where you are today.

Your short-term income issues are what we call liquidity— your ability to spend money immediately which will come from a few primary sources. First, you're going to have your monthly income sources that come in on a regular basis. That might be your salary, it might be a pension, and it might include Social Security benefits. You should also consider your bank accounts, your savings accounts and any life insurance proceeds. You will need to determine how you will pay your bills, things like your utilities, your insurances, any loans or mortgage or credit cards for at least the next few months.

You must also determine if your bills were previously paid electronically, whether they'll continue to be paid that way, and you need to make sure you have enough cash on hand to continue paying them. After you have the estimates of your monthly costs, you will need to determine how long your cash is likely going to last. Hopefully, you have at least a few months of cash available. Once you've got the short-term covered, you need to think about the long-term replacement of your income throughout your lifetime.

How are you going to do this? One way is to work full time or part time. Do you plan to work? Would you like to go back to work? Sometimes widows like to work because it helps occupy some of their time and avoid some of the loneliness.

Let's Start With Sources of Income

The following are primary sources to evaluate.

Social Security Benefits

As I mentioned earlier, young widows with children are sometimes eligible for Social Security which can ease some of the burden. Many times, Social Security benefits are available for widows, but how you collect those benefits can have dramatic long-term impacts. There are various strategies you can use, many are outside the scope of this book. The general rule is that a widow can collect the higher of her or her spouse's Social Security benefits. It may make sense for you to collect your benefits now and allow your spouse's to increase in the future or vice versa. It all depends on your individual situation. Again, professional help is really important because the Social Security employees are not typically equipped to help you make those decisions and are not permitted to provide advice.

Pensions

Was your deceased husband collecting a pension? If so, is there a survivor benefit? Most times, pension benefits have various survivorship options from lump sum payments, to payments for a certain number of years, to survivorship benefits where you'll continue the same payment that your spouse received. Determining this is important. Hopefully, there's a 100% survivorship benefit that allows you to continue the same payments that he was entitled to during his life.

Sometimes people are entitled to pensions in the future (called frozen pensions), but have not yet elected to receive them. Some companies terminate pension plans or people terminate jobs and their pensions are not payable until a later time, typically, at age 65. Again, you need to determine how much of your spouse's pension you are entitled to, and when.

Annuities

The term "annuity" may have many meanings. I will discuss only the type of annuity in the "payout" or annuitization phase. This means that the insurance company issuing the annuity pays a steady stream of income to the owner on a periodic basis, usually monthly. Any guarantees provided are based on the claims-paying ability of the issuing company.

Annuities typically offer various payout options designed to suit the income needs of individual or couples. Many annuities have payout options for a certain number of years, or for a lifetime. Oftentimes, an annuity owner will provide for survivorship payments. These survivorship payments, if any, depend on the individual elections selected at the time of annuitization. Survivorship options may be:

- A lump sum payment, called a Cash Refund option;
- A lifetime survivorship option, where the beneficiary (usually the spouse) collects all, or a portion, of the payments for their lifetime;
- A period of years, called a Period Certain, where the beneficiary collects all, or a portion, of the payments for a predetermined number of years.

Contacting the insurance company will be a big help in understanding your benefits, and to have them paid to you.

IRAs and Qualified Retirement Plans

There are a few different primary types of retirement plans, each with different tax characteristics. First, there are IRAs and qualified plans. Usually the money in these plans has never been taxed and is only taxed upon withdrawal. This allows the use of income tax minimization techniques to control your taxable income well into the future. At age 72, the IRS has Required Mandatory Distributions that must be withdrawn from these accounts, otherwise, you face a 50% IRS penalty on the amount that should have been withdrawn.

Roth IRAs are accounts funded by contributions that have already been taxed and allow tax-free growth* potential. They do not require distributions at age 72 and widows can transfer them to their own name. In many cases, you will want to leave money in these accounts as long as possible.

In some cases, younger spouses can transfer their spouses' IRAs or qualified plans into a beneficiary IRA if they are not yet 59½ to avoid any early withdrawal penalties. As noted above, the beneficiary designations on the individual accounts determine where those assets go. The flexibility to plan is much greater if, in fact, the beneficiaries are designated.

**Unless certain criteria are met, Roth IRA owners must be 59½ or older and have held the IRA for five years before tax-free withdrawals are permitted.*

Taxable Investment Portfolios

Taxable investment portfolios include stocks, bonds, mutual funds, and brokerage accounts. These accounts can generate taxable income each year, and can also fluctuate in value. To tax gains on the individual portfolio investments, investment firms (at the IRS' direction) account for what is called "cost basis" for each investment. This cost basis assures that any gains are subject to income tax only once. When an account owner dies, each investment's cost basis may be adjusted (in whole or in part) to its value on the date of death, called a step-up. This is something that can be updated and has the potential to lower taxable gains when the investment is eventually sold.

Regardless of which types of accounts you own, the order in which the accounts are liquidated (i.e. decumulated), can have a dramatic impact. This is the tax planning aspect of retirement income planning and is very difficult to do yourself. Over time tax laws are sure to change which further complicates matters. You may be wondering is how you can do all of this. I can't stress enough getting a professional to help you manage these issues.

In the next section, we will discuss wealth management planning and how it can benefit you and your family.

CHAPTER SEVEN: CHALLENGES THAT PREVENT FINANCIAL SUCCESS

"The price of inaction is far greater than the cost of making a mistake."
—Meister Eckhart, German Philosopher

We previously discussed some of the key emotional behaviors that can hinder your goals, and unlike emotional behaviors, financial issues are much easier to address. Now, let's discuss some of the specific financial issues you will be facing and the ways in which you can overcome them.

Many of the widows I work with want the following: A comfortable lifestyle now and in retirement. They don't want to change the standard of living to which they are accustomed, and they want to be able to spend time with their families. Next, they want financial independence. They don't want to be a financial burden to their kids, friends, or relatives.

We mentioned earlier that widows tend to let money worries consume their whole life and with good reason. What you need to remember is you should continue to enjoy your life. If you properly budget, you will have a good idea of what you can spend monthly or annually. It doesn't mean you can take private jets around the world but, hopefully, you'll be able to enjoy the same lifestyle you had while your spouse was alive.

Let's discuss some of the financial problems that prevent success, how to correct them, and what you can do to increase your chances. Be proactive in all that you do, and break the planning into manageable pieces. Remember, a journey of a thousand miles, begins with a single step. So, let's keep it simple. I can't stress enough that lowering the complexity of your financial affairs will allow you to comprehend your situation. This understanding will give you more confidence, and that confidence will result in better decision-making.

Here are the top 5 challenges that may prevent financial success:

1. Lack of Awareness

One financial issue for widows can be a lack of awareness. Life is complicated. Today, we have Smartphones, computers and the internet, yet people don't even want to take the time or energy to educate themselves and hook up their computer which comes with color-coded cables. What people tend to focus on are their daily tasks and the complexity of life … of daily life. The result is they fail to pay attention to their finances because they figure they would just worry about them "tomorrow." Nobody notices the day-to-day changes because they're subtle. You look in the mirror every day, and nothing really ever seems to change; but if you look at a picture of yourself from 10 years ago, you probably looked a lot better back then. Most people are unaware of this and tend to wait until it's too difficult or impossible to fix. Knowledge and understanding allows you to take a broader look at the situation, and to be more proactive.

2. Failing to Plan

There's an old adage, "If you fail to plan, you plan to fail." Again, you have to determine where you are financially today, where you want to go and what you want to do. Then you need to fill in the gaps and identify the potential problems along the way that you may face. Unfortunately, you probably aren't aware of many of these potential problems. You must always remember that inflation and longevity go hand-in-hand and what seemed like a lifetime of money may, in fact, not be enough. You will have to determine how much you're going to need in today's dollars and then project these costs well into the future. Remember, at 3% inflation, your cost of living is going to double every 24 years. Without properly projecting these costs, how are you ever going to know if your wealth is sufficient to maintain your lifestyle? So, you need to evaluate your retirement savings and then ask yourself, "Have I saved enough for my retirement? Am I spending too much and will I have enough money to be financially independent?"

3. Family Members and Friends

Another challenge to financial success can be family members and friends who want to help with your finances. Very few family members have had sufficient training in wealth management. They may be a convenient source for you, but may not be a sensible one. One key problem is that your emotional impact doubles since they are emotionally involved in one way or another. What if they make a mistake? The emotional pressure increases for the entire family. My experience is that having a family member manage your affairs is rarely a good option. Incidentally, I have several clients who have family who are investment professionals, yet they do not want their financial affairs to interfere with their family dynamics. My advice is to turn a scenario like this into a positive.

To do this, encourage the family or friends to attend the wealth management meetings with you. A few years ago, a recent widow came to see me about her financial affairs. As a courtesy, her sister-in-law and brother-in-law joined our meeting (from 3,000 miles away), just to make sure she would not be taken advantage of. The reason I tell you the story is that sometimes, bringing the kids or relatives allows all your concerned parties to hear the same story, which can result in a collective confidence in the process (i.e., two heads are better than one). I find the kids and relatives all want to be involved only until they know that mom's taken care of. I think it's a great way to turn a negative into a positive.

4. The 6 0'Clock News Is Not Your Money Manager

Managing a portfolio is complicated. There are thousands of investment products from which to choose. Do you pick one investment or do you spread them out and use multiple firms, or do you use multiple advisors? Then you've got the ever-present media barrage. When was the last time you heard a news blurb, "Everything's just fine in the market, tune in at 11?" You probably never have and never will. The media's real job is not to provide useful information; instead, they want you to watch their television programs so they can sell more advertisements.

The emotional issues (discussed in the earlier chapters) tend to be magnified by the media. This creates a dangerous combination of a lack of education and a lot of emotion, increasing the potential for bad decision-making. There are countless studies and statistics about the devastating effects of buying and selling at the wrong time. Since the beginning of the millennium, the investment markets have been very volatile and have created an environment ripe for bad decision-making. Combining these market ups and downs with constant, negative media attention about how bad things are in the world makes matters even more difficult.

5. Not Enough Time

Another issue is not having enough time. This is the probably the most common problem. Too often people ask, "Why would I do something today that I can put off until tomorrow?" The lifestyles we live today are complicated, they're fast-paced and we all seem too busy. Newly retired clients constantly say they don't know how they had time to work. We're spending time with our kids, our grandkids, going to soccer games, going to their plays. We live a very mobile lifestyle, far more mobile than years ago. The result is that planning gets put on the back burner. People don't have the time today to properly focus on their investments, their asset allocation, the retirement planning, their taxes, and all other facets of their financial lives.

The good news is that you can do something about these issues if you're motivated and you receive the proper advice and guidance.

CHAPTER EIGHT: PROFESSIONAL ADVICE

"Risk comes from not knowing what you are doing."
—Warren Buffett

So far, we've discussed some of the issues that may affect your financial situation, like inflation and longevity. We've also discussed the emotional issues and additional financial hurdles you may be facing. If you're still reading at this point, you probably agree you need some help.

You may be asking yourself, where do I find the right financial advisor? First, you need to know what you're looking for, and then you need to know where to look. For many years, widows have articulated that they want and need a trusted advisor they can turn to, to get straight, objective advice. They're looking for an advocate who will digest all of the complexity the financial markets bring, and then help them make proper long-term decisions consistent with their goals.

A very seasoned attorney once told me, "Son, you will know you are a great attorney, not when you know all the answers, but when you know all the right questions to ask." In order to properly guide you, an advisor will need to invest a lot of time to understand your individual, emotional, and financial situation. This is best accomplished by asking thoughtful questions to determine your true feelings. Only then, can the advisor create a plan of action to address and solve your problems. In future years, he or she will continue to adjust your plan to accommodate the changes that are certain to occur. As I suggested earlier in the book, most widows prefer to have a Personal Financial Coach; someone who will help them make all types of sound long-term financial decisions. They want someone who is client-centric, looking out for their best interests and not simply trying to sell investment products. They also want a relationship they can depend on for many years into the future.

Types of Financial Advice

Understanding the different types of advice available may help you better understand your options. Let me explain how financial consultants vary along with the services they provide. There are two primary types of financial advisors: those who manage investments and those who manage wealth.

Investment Consultants

Typically, Investment Consultants offer a broad range of investment products and provide investment management services. This is the primary function for many, if not all, financial consultants. In many cases, their advice and services are geared toward providing and managing your portfolio.

Wealth Managers

Wealth Managers, on the other hand take a more comprehensive, holistic approach to your needs. Their advice goes far beyond just the management of your portfolio. Instead, they focus on your goals, and what you want to accomplish. This requires a deep understanding of you, your family and what you want to accomplish.

Wealth Managers use a highly consultative approach that begins with gaining a deep comprehension of the various financial issues you currently face, and those you are likely to face in the future. Ask yourself, "Do I want someone managing my portfolio who doesn't know everything about me?"

As you might imagine, Wealth Management Planning requires a substantial time commitment, consistent communication, and ongoing discipline both for you and the Advisor. In our ever-changing world, Wealth Managers need to continuously reeducate themselves on issues well beyond the capital markets. They also need to be well-versed in the areas of estate planning, tax and insurance. This is one of the many reasons Wealth Managers may seem more difficult to find.

Wealth Managers' broad financial planning knowledge allows them to coordinate your affairs with your other team of professionals. Once they have identified your goals and needs, they work with your team of advisors (i.e. CPA, attorney) to assist them in designing custom strategies to meet your (and your family's) needs. Note that this advice will not be static and instead will change as your personal situation and regulations change in the future. These regular contacts and meetings help increase the probability that your planning remains current. Doing so also improves the likelihood of your long-term financial success.

Isn't this what you would envision when you think of your Personal Financial Coach?

To begin the process of finding your Personal Financial Coach, you should arm yourself with appropriate questions to ask. Below are a few that may help you better pre-screen potential candidates.

Chart 3: Steps to Help You Select an Advisor
1. Do they have a clean record? You can check in the Broker section (brokercheck.finra.org) of FINRA's Website (www.FINRA.org) or the Advisor section (adviserinfo.sec.gov) of the SEC Website (www.SEC.gov).
2. Do they seem interested in getting to know you, or is their emphasis mostly on the products they sell?
3. Some advisors work on commission, others for fees, and some use a mix. These are all acceptable – just make sure advisors are upfront about their compensation methods.
4. Do the advisors have many different kinds of products available, or do they try to solve all problems with just one or two kinds?
5. Do the advisors work with other clients who are in the same net worth category as you?
6. Do they seem to understand you and your specific problems and issues?
7. Are they concerned about what is important to you and your family?

The Consultative Process

Now armed with some basic knowledge (and questions), hopefully, you are feeling an increased level of confidence. You are probably asking how a financial advisor can actually make all this happen. In order to get to know you and your goals, and then structure a plan you can understand, the advisor will need to employ a consultative process. Most people I have interviewed become more comfortable when a process is implemented to help manage all of their financial and wealth management needs. I recommend you find an advisor who will surround himself or herself with a team of other professionals experienced in handling a variety of specialties, such as estate planning or tax counselling. Portfolio management should only be part of your advisor's responsibility.

Here is what you should be looking for in an advisor, and here is how they do it. To simplify what a consultative process might look like, let me use a formula to help explain how this is accomplished.

Consultative Process = IC + AP + RM

The Consultative Process combines Investment Consulting (IC) with Advanced Planning (AP) and Relationship Management (RM).

Investment Consulting

Investment consulting is a core competency of most financial advisors. An advisor will evaluate a client's risk tolerance and then customize a portfolio that's going to match their needs as written in a custom Investment Policy Statement (the "IPS"). When there's a process in place, your customized investment plan can be simplified and explained in terms you can understand. When you understand how and why your portfolio is structured the way it is, you're far more apt to stick with it, especially during difficult financial times.

Advanced Planning

Advanced Planning has its own sub-formula. That is:

AP = WE + WT + WP + CG

Advanced Planning is comprised of Wealth Enhancement (WE), Wealth Transfer (WT), Wealth Protection (WP) and Charitable Giving (CG).

Advanced Planning is the part of the consultative process beyond simple investment consulting advice. Wealth enhancement first includes tax planning and strives to reduce taxes as much as reasonably possible. It also details cash flow and retirement income planning in addition to your customized financial plan that's updated year after year.

Wealth Transfer involves determining who you want to receive your assets and then preparing an efficient plan to have that occur. In most cases, you'll need to work with an attorney to prepare your estate plan, which will be coordinated by your advisor.

The Wealth Protection function is to prevent your assets from being unjustly taken and to mitigate some of the risks you face in daily life. For most, it includes having adequate property and casualty insurance, including umbrella or excess liability coverage. Trying to protect yourself from Identity Theft should also be addressed.

Charitable Giving is becoming more and more popular every year with successful families. Planning properly during your lifetime can help benefit you, your families and the charities most important to you, while providing adequate tax benefits.

Relationship Management

Relationship Management consists of two separate functions. First, within a consultative process, your advisor is going to take the time to know you to understand what you're trying to accomplish. As your needs change, your plans will change. They know this because they will meet regularly with you, usually two to four times per year to discuss all aspects of your financial affairs.

Another important aspect of Relationship Management refers to your network of other professional advisors, such as attorneys, accountants and insurance agents. If you don't already have these relationships in place, your advisor will introduce you to outside professionals experienced in Advanced Planning matters like yours. Working in conjunction with these professionals almost always has positive effects. Two heads are typically better than one.

In Summary

After reading this book, I hope you appreciate the value of having a Personal Financial Coach, and how he or she will benefit you in making more informed decisions about your money. While you can't eliminate all the external forces that are going to affect you over the next several decades, having a wealth management relationship should increase the probability of you achieving your goals. Hopefully, you're going to avoid major mistakes, you're going to plan properly, and you're going to do so with far less emotion and with someone to help guide you.

I am confident that if you follow the concepts outlined and work with professionals who have your best interests at heart, you will have a much better plan to reach your financial destination. If you have made notes about your concerns and challenges, and have a clear view of the type of professionals you want to work with, you will have the confidence to make sound financial decisions for your future with your trusted advisor.

EPILOGUE

I truly hope you enjoyed the book and I'm certain it will help provide confidence either for your future planning or after your husband's passing. You may have already experienced some of the emotional issues firsthand; recognizing their effects should be helpful. In addition, you will realize your feelings are perfectly normal. Just remember that what you feel, and what you will go through over the coming months, can be conquered with patience, planning and professional help. Keeping your goals in perspective, and keeping things "simple" will give you confidence in your decisions and will prevent second-guessing.

You are going to face numerous obstacles along the way. You can either fall down (Investment Paralysis), or pick yourself up by the bootstraps (Plan). I once experienced a widow who, for years, was devastated by the loss of her husband. She suffered from investment paralysis for years until one day; out of the blue she sent me a letter stating that she was changing her life.

"I used to live in fear. I now do not accept those thoughts. I refuse to dwell on hurts, worries, fears, and negatives. I used to wonder if there was a God. I thought of myself as a nobody. I have learned to value myself and not worry about what others think or say. I have replaced my bad thoughts with praising and thanking God and since I talk to God a lot, I feel closer to Him. God always seemed so far away and so silent. I do not dwell on "what ifs" and "if only's" in life. I totally trust God and now with conquered fears through faith in His promise to take care of my tomorrows. My husband used to say "Roll with the punches;" I'm learning. I read the bible and pray every day."

She no longer lived in fear. She would manage both her personal and financial lives to make the most of them. She was going to be financially independent and would not let her initial fears dictate how she managed her life. To this day, she is a completely different person and has never looked back. Sometimes, you just have to find your inner and spiritual strength.

Please take what I have learned (from the school of hard knocks) from my involvement in the financial and legal worlds, and use it to protect yourself. Try to plan ahead so you can prevent so many of the common mistakes I see on a daily basis. One of my dad's long-time friends had a saying, "If a dog bites you twice, you're dumber than the dog." The best way to protect yourself is by getting unbiased, professional help in managing your affairs.

If you have never worked with an advisor, understand and quantify how much their advice will cost and balance it against the value you will receive. Please do not underestimate or overlook how an experienced professional can help you understand common investment mistakes and save you time and trouble managing your affairs.

If you have an advisor, ask yourself whether you are getting proper wealth management advice. If not, do yourself a favor, and please have the courage to search for the "right" advisor. All too often, I meet widows who are uncomfortable with their advisors (usually salespeople) who knew they were not getting sound advice, but did not know where to turn. Would you go into open heart surgery with someone you did not feel comfortable with? If not, you would probably get a second opinion.

When you factor in the volatile markets we have experienced in the last several years, more widows are experiencing high levels of doubt and uncertainty. Many widows reevaluate their future expectations, causing them to question whether their current advisory relationship is right for themselves and their families. I advise widows to ask themselves some pointed questions:

- Are my goals and vision for the future in alignment with my current financial strategy and investments?
- Is my financial advisor reviewing my entire financial picture, including insurance, estate planning, tax mitigation, charitable giving and investing, to make sure I am making informed choices?
- Are my outside professional advisors in these key areas the right ones?
- Do they deeply understand me, and my family, and our unique situation?
- Have they structured an appropriate plan and are they working together as a team to execute it?

If you answered "no" to more than one of these, I suggest you seek a second opinion from an experienced wealth manager. Remember, what most widows want is a long-term relationship with an advisor who can provide professional, ongoing and long-term advice. What widows need is an advocate to help them achieve financial independence.

From my family to yours, all the best!

ABOUT THE AUTHOR: Paul L. Marrella

Paul L. Marrella is a Wealth Manager at Marrella Financial Group, LLC.

He focuses on providing wealth management solutions to successful families in Southeastern, Pennsylvania. Together with his father, brother and sister, he helps affluent clients address their five biggest concerns: preserving their wealth, mitigating taxes, taking care of their heirs, ensuring their assets are not unjustly taken, and charitable giving.

Along with his father, Paul A., he founded Marrella Financial Group, LLC in 2001. Paul and his family now serve more than 300 families and institutions who have entrusted assets of more than $300 million. He uses a consultative process to gain a detailed understanding of his clients' deepest values and goals. He then employs customized recommendations designed to address each client's unique needs and aspirations well beyond simply investments.

Successful families work with Paul to:

- Develop and implement a comprehensive wealth management plan to help them reach their financial goals.
- Make smarter decisions in today's uncertain political, economic and social environment.
- Obtain an independent Second Opinion from an experienced financial advisor in their community.

Early in his career, Paul was an attorney with the law firm of Fry & Golden specializing in estate planning and administration. He also spent several years on Wall Street as an equity trader with Spear, Leeds & Kellogg. In 1998, Paul re-joined his father's practice where he uses his diverse experience to help clients navigate today's complicated retirement landscape. He also acts as his firm's managing partner.

He is a noted public speaker on financial issues affecting retirees. He is also an active board member of several non-profit organization boards and is active in his local bar association. Paul was also active in youth sports, coaching over 25 seasons. In his spare time, he is an avid golfer and a black belt in Ryu Kyu Hon Kenpo Kobujitsu Karate.

FOOTNOTES:

1. "Leveling the Playing Field: Upgrading the Wealth Management Experience for Women", The Boston Consulting Group, Peter Damisch, Monish Kumar, Anna Zakrzewski & Natalia Zhinlinskaya, July 2010
2. https://www.bcg.com/publications/2020/managing-next-decade-women-wealth.aspx
3. https://www.ubs.com/content/dam/WealthManagementAmericas/documents/2018-37666-UBS-Own-Your-Worth-report-R32.pdf
4. https://www.barrons.com/articles/widowed-women-highlight-wealth-gap-between-genders-1543851956
5. OFFICE OF DISCIPLINARY COUNSEL v. JEFFREY J. HOWELL, No. 1635, Disciplinary Docket No. 3, No. 155 DB 2008
6. http://online.wsj.com/news/articles/SB10001424052970204190504577040402069714264?mg=reno64-wsj "Clients from Venus" Wall Street Journal, April 30, 2012
7. http://www.ssa.gov/OACT/population/longevity.html
8. http://www.socialsecurity.gov/OACT/STATS/table4c6.html
9. https://www.pgpf.org/blog/2019/05/healthcare-costs-for-americans-projected-to-grow-at-an-alarmingly-high-rate
10. https://www.fidelity.com/bin-public/060_www_fidelity_com/documents/press-release/healthcare-price-check-040219.pdf
11. https://www.ebri.org/docs/default-source/ebri-issue-brief/ebri_ib_481_savingstargets-16may19.pdf?sfvrsn=56b83f2f
12. https://www.genworth.com/aging-and-you/finances/cost-of-care.html

Made in United States
Cleveland, OH
05 November 2026

47764840R00048